Dear Reader,

We all need our own little BLUEPRINTS, or plans, in life. Sometimes making a plan is fun. Sometimes it's hard. Sometimes the plan doesn't work, so we make a new one. And sometimes, the plan is exactly what we need, just when we need it. As you read this Have a Plan Book, we hope you will ask questions, talk about it with family and friends, and create your very own plan. You can do this on your own or together with a grown-up.

Your plan may grow and change each time you read your book, and that's great! As life happens, plans change. But remember, having a little Blueprint is always helpful, in difficult times and in good times. So go ahead: BLUEPRINT IT!

Lovingly,

Your friends at little BLUEPRINT

P.S. Children and adults around the world are making their own little BLUEPRINTS. If you want to see the plans of others, or share yours, just go to

www.littleBLUEPRINT.com

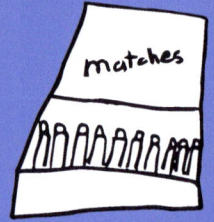

HAVE A PLAN Books

To purchase a hardcover or
personalized version of any
little BLUEPRINT book,
with names, optional photo(s),
and details, please go to:

www.littleBLUEPRINT.com

The author would like to thank,
for all of their support and expertise:
Dan Siegel, M.D.;
Nina Shapiro, M.D.;
Pattie Fitzgerald
(Founder of Safely Ever After, Inc., www.safelyeverafter.com); and
my editors, Leslie Budnick and Gina Shaw.
A special thanks to:
Phoebe, age 10, for her blueprint illustration; and
Lexi, age 7, for her title page illustration.

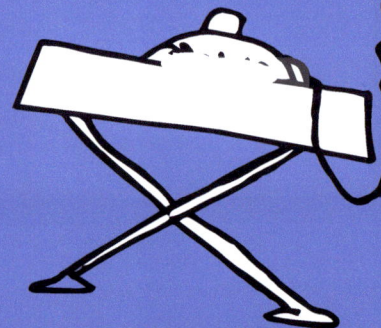

TO BE SAFE

at Home,

I HAVE A PLAN

by Katherine Eskovitz

illustrated by Jessica Churchill

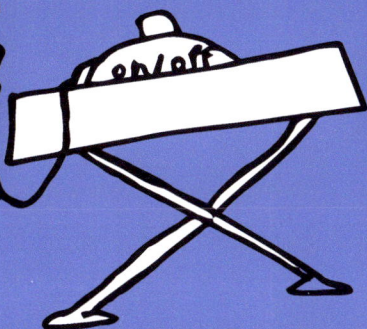

I love playing at home. There is an expression,

"I FEEL AT HOME,"

because home is where we feel comfortable and loved.

That is why we call it
Home Sweet Home.

SAFETY PLAN:

- Fire
- Just in case drills
- Hot and sharp objects
- Chemicals
- Electricity
- Dial 911

I AM SAFE AT HOME.

Being **SAFE** means I am not in danger,

and I do not get hurt.

I stay safe because my parents
and others help keep me safe.

NEWS ALERT:

*Children are home
safety helpers!*

TO BE SAFE
at Home

I HAVE A PLAN

I can also help everyone stay safe when having fun at home by following **SOME SIMPLE SAFETY RULES.**

STAYING SAFE means learning how to be prepared for situations that will probably never happen, but it is always smart to be ready, just in case.

I always look forward to **BIRTHDAY CELEBRATIONS** at home.
An adult lights the birthday candles, and everyone sings,
"Happy Birthday to You!"

TO **STAY SAFE** WHILE ENJOYING CELEBRATIONS,

I can help make sure that nobody ever plays with FIRE.

Smart safety helpers do not light matches or candles without an adult.

BE SAFE: NEVER PLAY WITH MATCHES, CANDLES, OR FIRE.

I love the smell of cookies baking in the oven. YUM! It's fun to learn how to measure ingredients and to stir the batter.

A smart safety helper will make sure nobody touches HOT pot handles or gets their clothes too close to the stove.

If paper or fabric is too close to heat, IT COULD LIGHT ON FIRE.
I should make sure nobody leaves a shirt draped over a lamp
or a potholder on a stove.

I can be a helper by making sure everyone keeps their
HANDS, CLOTHES, AND HAIR AWAY FROM HEAT.

BE SAFE: KEEP OUR BODY AND FABRIC AWAY FROM HEAT.

Although it will probably never happen,

if our hair or clothing should catch on fire,

STOP

DROP

and ROLL.

That's easy to say and easy to remember. STOPPING our body prevents a fire from spreading; DROPPING to the ground and covering our face keeps us from getting burned; and ROLLING on a carpet or the ground helps put out the fire quickly.

We have **FIRE DRILLS** at school to practice safety,
and it is smart for our family to practice safety at home, too.

I can help my family plan how to

LEAVE OUR HOME QUICKLY and

PICK AN OUTSIDE MEETING SPOT

for any emergency.

BE SAFE: HAVE A FAMILY PLAN FOR AN EMERGENCY.

It's fun to do arts and crafts projects at home.

Scissors were first used thousands of years ago in Ancient Egypt.

I AM ALWAYS CAREFUL WITH SHARP OBJECTS

because I do not want to cut myself or anyone else.

That would hurt!

I can be a safety helper and make sure nobody ever runs

with a sharp object or leaves it where someone might sit.

When handing scissors to someone else,

I make sure to pass the scissors handle first.

BE SAFE: BE CAREFUL WHEN HANDLING SHARP OBJECTS.

Vincent Van Gogh was a Dutch painter who lived over 100 years ago. Artists long ago did not know that putting paint in their mouth could be dangerous.

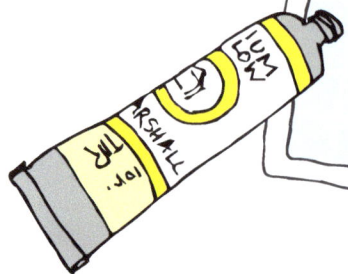

While painting is a great activity to do at home,
some paints, cleaning supplies, and medicine can be POISONOUS,
which means they can hurt us if we swallow them.

As a helper, I can make sure make sure no one ever puts
anything on or in their body unless we are told it is safe—
NOT IN OUR MOUTH, NOT IN OUR EARS, NOT IN OUR NOSE.

BE SAFE: NEVER PUT ANYTHING IN OUR MOUTH UNLESS
WE ARE ABSOLUTELY SURE IT IS SAFE TO EAT.
ALWAYS ASK A GROWN-UP FIRST WHEN UNSURE.

Thanks to electricity,
we can have fun family nights
watching an old family video or movie.
ELECTRICITY is a helpful form of energy that powers the
TELEVISION, LIGHTS, COMPUTERS,
and lots of other things.

In the 1700s, Ben Franklin used a metal key tied to a kite to prove that lightning was a stream of electricity. He understood that lightning was dangerous so he invented the lightning rod to keep buildings safe from fire by sending lightning strikes through a metal rod to the ground. ZAP!

Appliances have safe cords and coverings to keep us from touching the electricity inside the appliance.

Electricity travels in metal and in water.

Because our body has water inside of it, electricity could travel into our bodies and hurt us if we touch it.

So I can help make sure nobody ever sticks their fingers, tools, or toys in an electrical outlet, toaster, or any other electrical appliance.

Electricity and water are not safe together;

Safety helpers keep electrical appliances such as
HAIR DRYERS and MUSIC PLAYERS away from water,
especially the sink, bath, and shower.

BE SAFE: KEEP ELECTRICITY OUT OF OUR BODY BY
KEEPING ELECTRICITY AWAY FROM
OUR FINGERS, METAL OBJECTS, AND WATER.

We are safe because our parents and
others help keep us safe,

and because we know safety rules, too.

We are also safe because there are awesome

POLICE, FIREFIGHTERS, and

PARAMEDICS—people who work on ambulances—

who come quickly to help us if we dial 911 in an emergency.

On March 10, 1876, Alexander Graham Bell made the first telephone call for help while testing his invention of a phone.

If there is an emergency and no adult is available,
I can be a hero and dial **911**
to get help right away.

When calling 911, I will be asked what is happening and the address of where I am, so help can come quickly.

I can memorize my parents'
NAMES, ADDRESS, and PHONE NUMBER(S)
(so I can call them wherever they are).

NAMES:

_____

_____

ADDRESS:

_____

_____

PHONE NUMBER(S):

_____

_____

BE SAFE: DIAL 911 IN AN EMERGENCY AND KNOW
MY PARENTS' CONTACT INFORMATION.

I have many people who keep me safe every day. I can be a safety helper by making my own safety plan, together with my family, using the ideas in this book.

I love being safe in my Home Sweet Home!

SAMPLE PLAN

1. BE SAFE: NEVER PLAY WITH MATCHES, CANDLES, OR FIRE.

2. BE SAFE: KEEP OUR BODY AND FABRIC AWAY FROM HEAT.

3. BE SAFE: HAVE A FAMILY PLAN FOR AN EMERGENCY.

4. BE SAFE: BE CAREFUL WHEN HANDLING SHARP OBJECTS.

5. BE SAFE: NEVER PUT ANYTHING IN OUR MOUTH UNLESS WE ARE ABSOLUTELY SURE IT IS SAFE TO EAT. ALWAYS ASK A GROWN-UP FIRST WHEN UNSURE.

6. BE SAFE: KEEP ELECTRICITY OUT OF OUR BODY BY KEEPING ELECTRICITY AWAY FROM OUR FINGERS, METAL OBJECTS, AND WATER.

7. BE SAFE: DIAL 911 IN AN EMERGENCY AND KNOW MY PARENTS' CONTACT INFORMATION.

Here is MY PLAN

www.littleBLUEPRINT.com

Check out other children's BLUEPRINTS from around the world and share yours, too!

Other titles in the
HAVE A PLAN Series

WHEN IT'S TIME FOR BED, I HAVE A PLAN

TO CELEBRATE THE HOLIDAYS, I HAVE A PLAN

WHEN I MISS SOMEONE SPECIAL, I HAVE A PLAN

WHEN I MISS MY SPECIAL PET, I HAVE A PLAN

WHEN MY PARENTS DIVORCE, I HAVE A PLAN

TO BE SAFE ON THE GO, I HAVE A PLAN

TO KEEP MY BODY SAFE, I HAVE A PLAN

TO BE A HEALTHY EATER, I HAVE A PLAN

WHEN MY PARENTS SEPARATE, I HAVE A PLAN

AND MORE

New titles added regularly at

www.littleBLUEPRINT.com

All titles are available ready-made and personalized

little
BLUEPRINT
Empowering children. Training the brain.
WWW.LITTLEBLUEPRINT.COM

www.ingramcontent.com/pod-product-compliance
Lightning Source LLC
LaVergne TN
LVHW072101070426
835508LV00002B/210